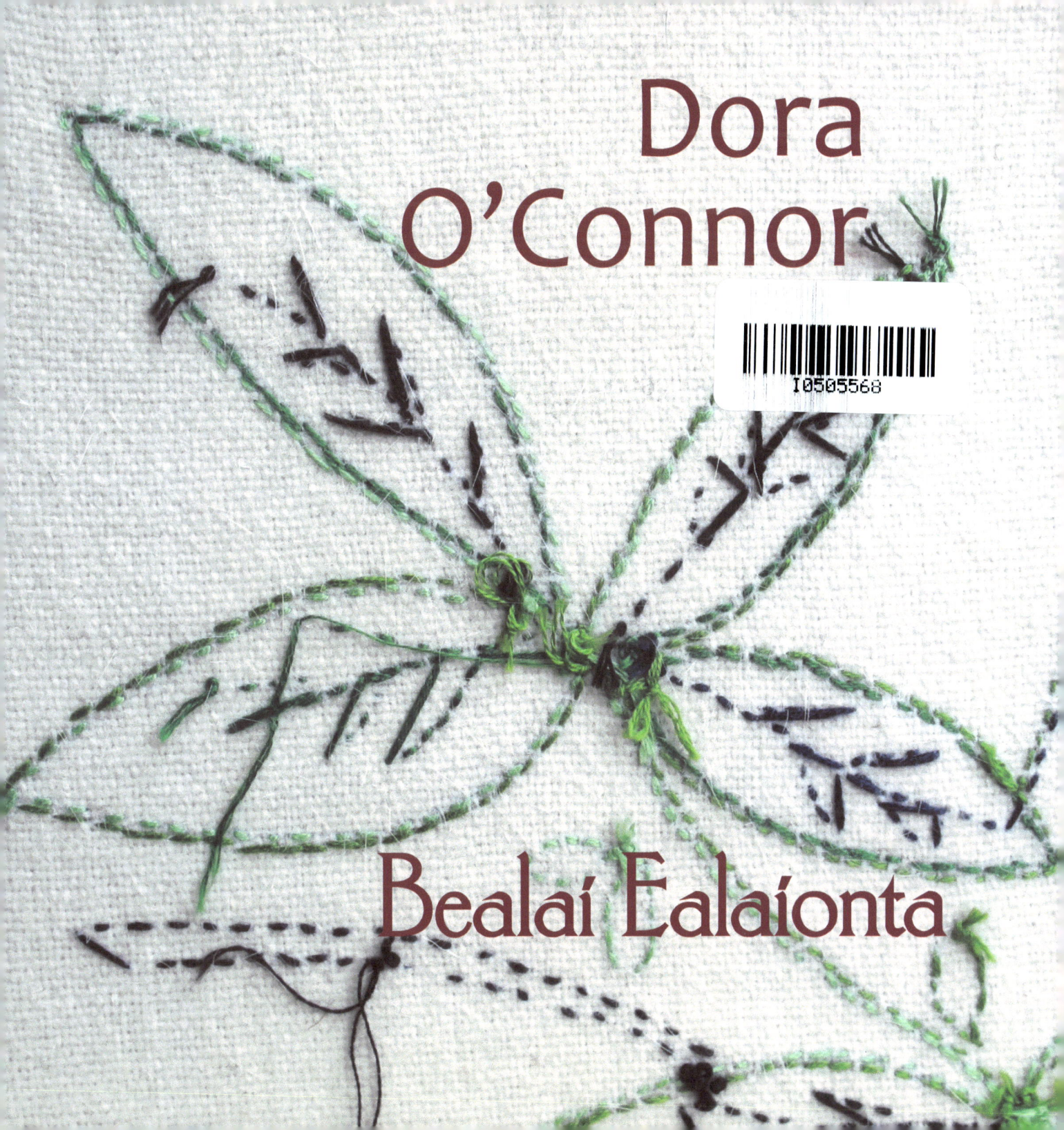

Dora O'Connor

Bealaí Ealaíonta

Bealaí Ealaíonta
(Artful Paths)

Text by
Dora O'Connor
as told to
Kristi Collins

Photographs by
Úna Ní Shé

Design by
Kristi Collins and Úna Ní Shé

Layout by
Kristi Collins

Artwork by
Dora O'Connor

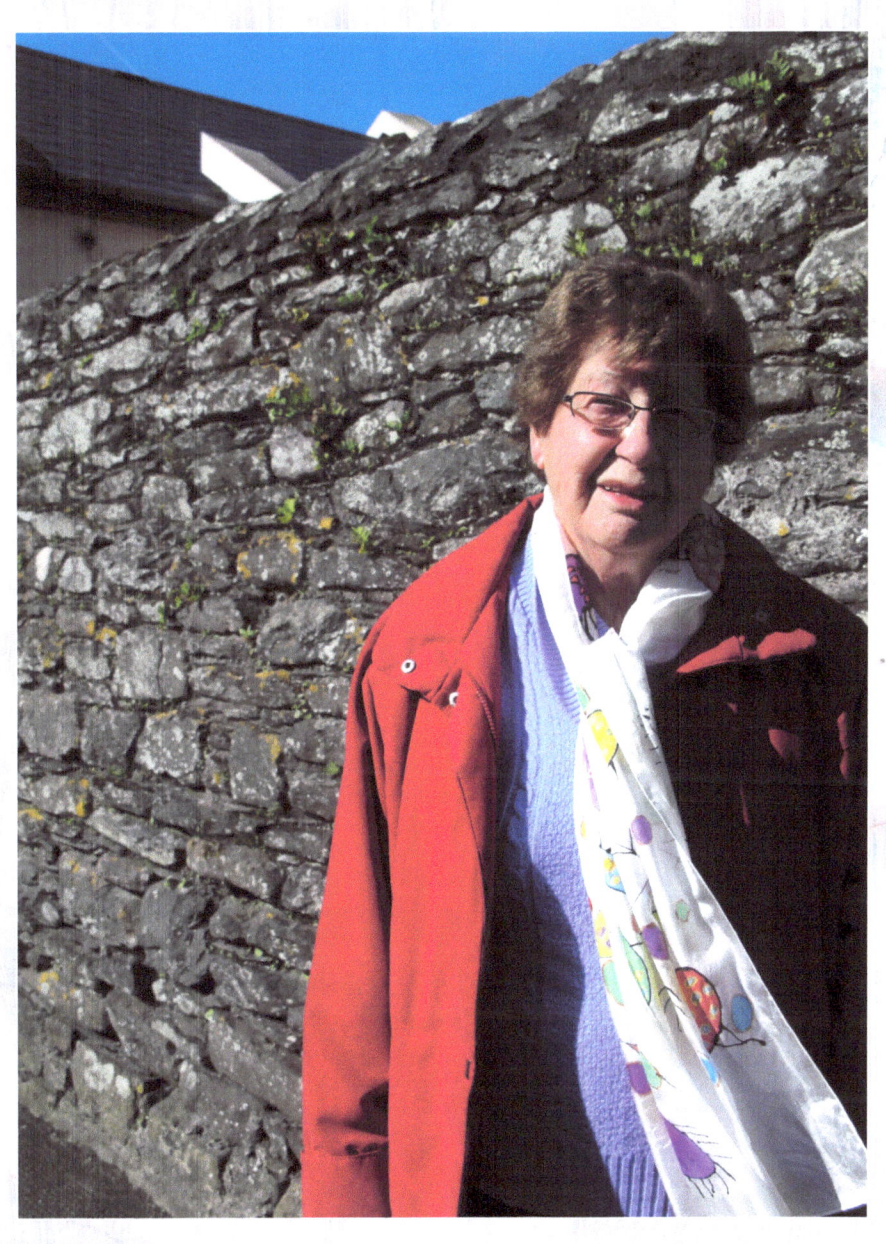

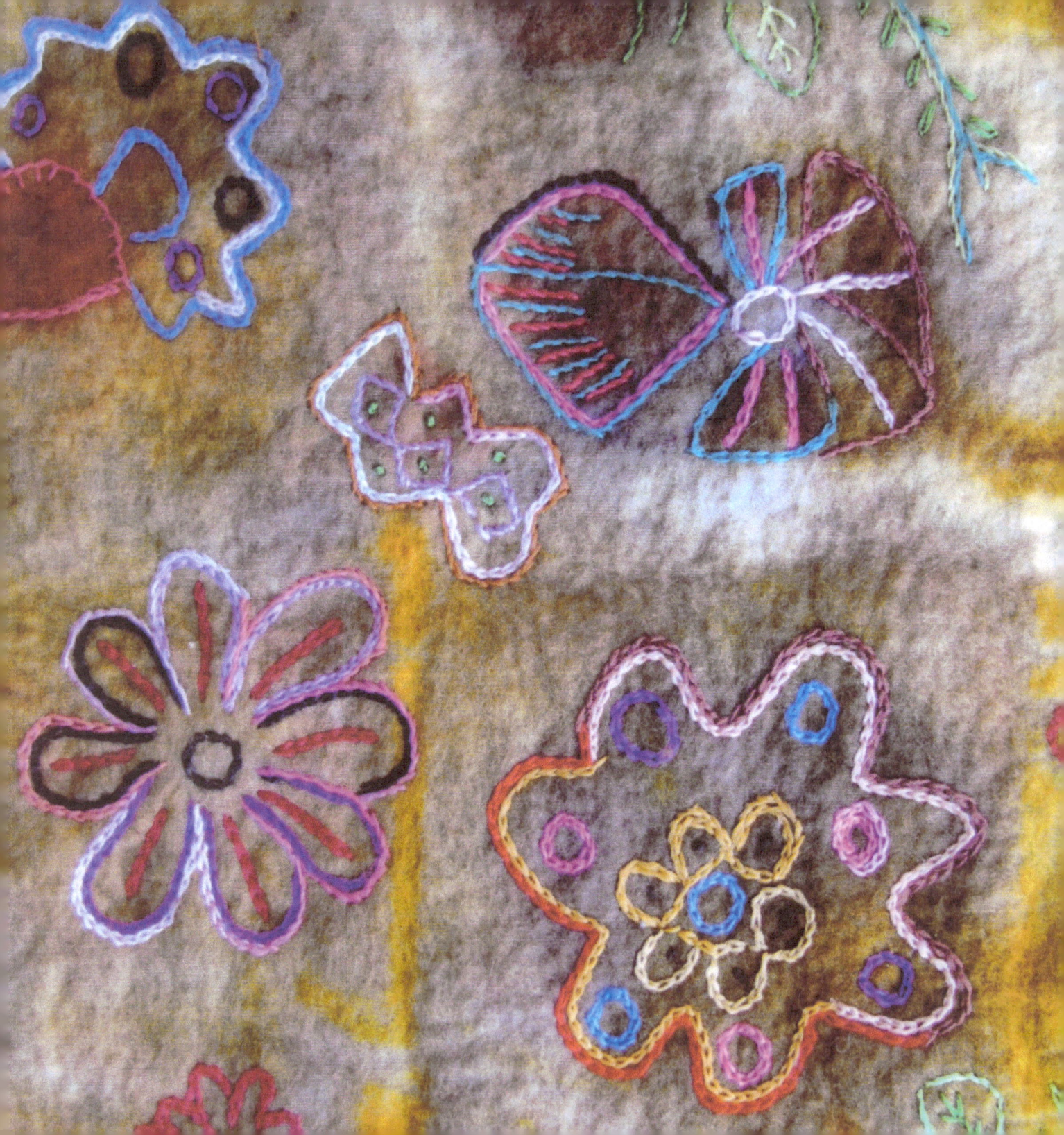

My mother was good for the sewing.
She made lots of clothes from when we were young.
You couldn't afford to buy them at that time, so you had
to make them, and I learned it from her.
We'd take old dresses belonging to the older ones,
rip them up and make them smaller; that's how it was at
that time. I always worked off a pattern, but I don't
know that she did.

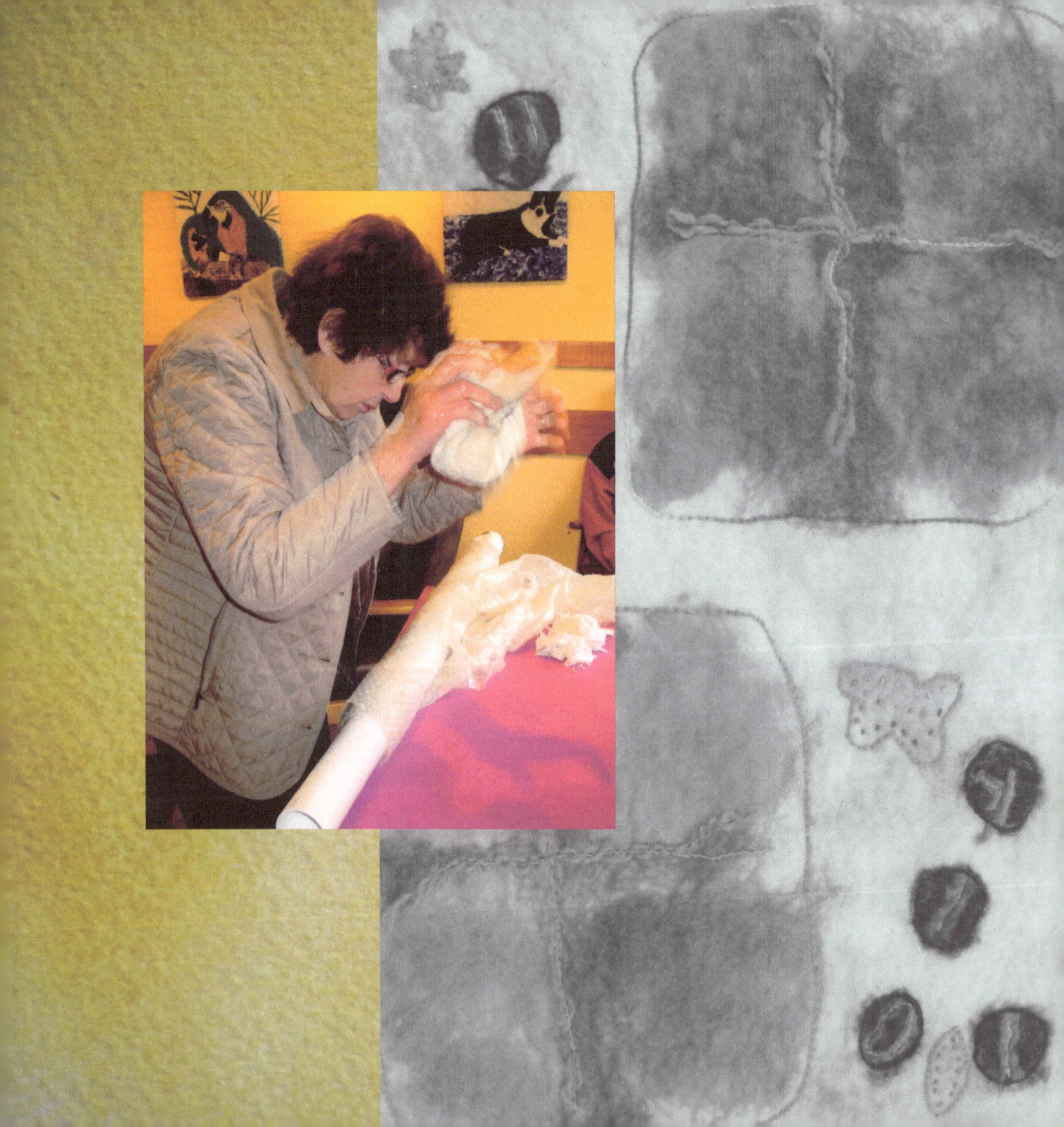

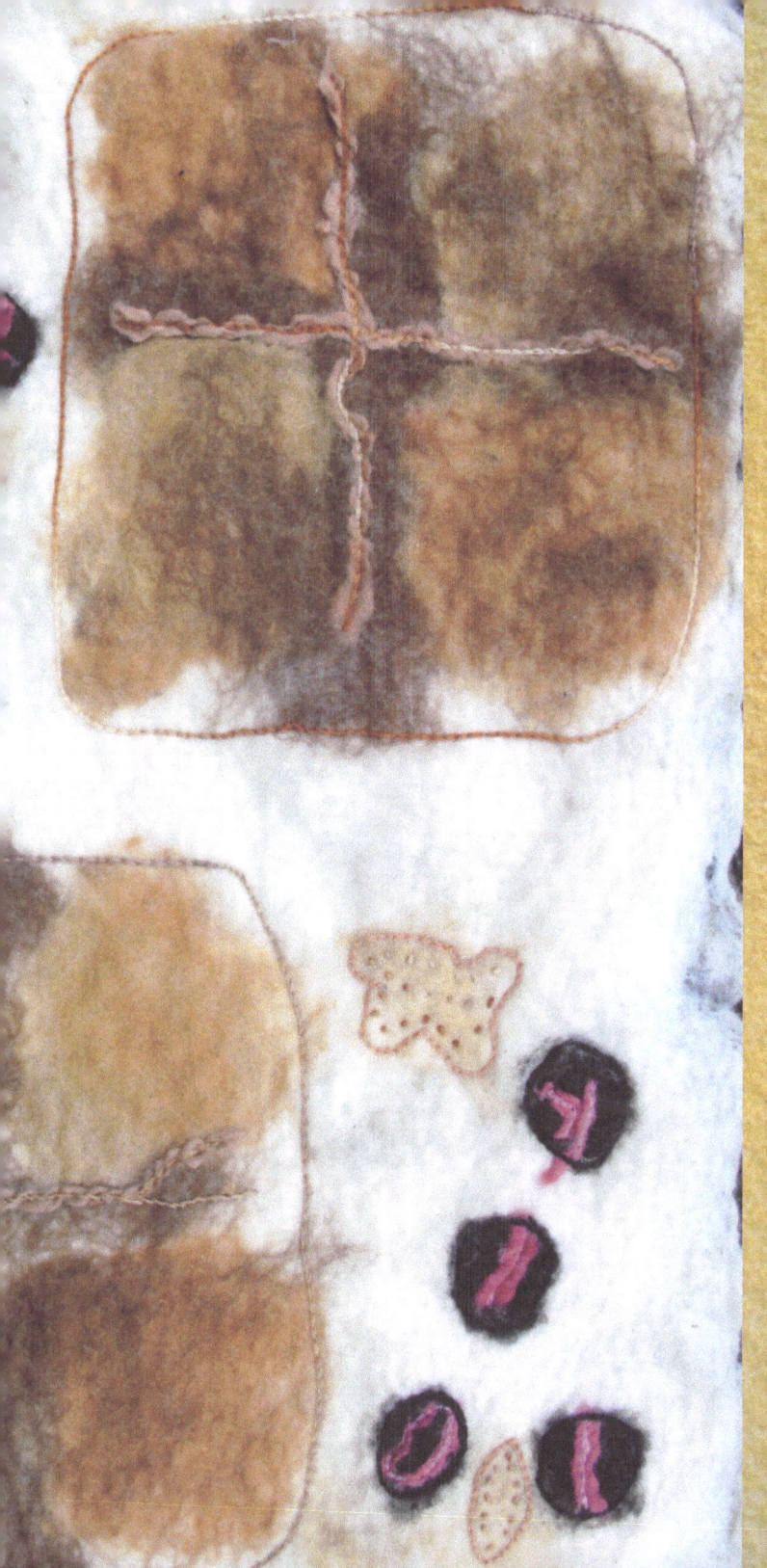

Recipe for Currant Loaf

The plain currant loaf, you make it with flour
four cups of flour now say, four cups
four ounces of margarine
a bit of oil, and nutmeg and sugar
I use my fist for the sugar
don't ever measure anything
Buttermilk,
currants and sultanas
baking powder, or soda
and you mix them all together
with the buttermilk, and maybe an egg
Make a dough, and put in in to bake.

Long ago we had the open fire
and we had to put coals on top
Did you never see that?
Coals on top of the oven
and you'd hang the loaf in an oven
and put the cover on it
and put the coals out of the fire on top
to bake the loaf.
The pie used to be made in the oven too
that time, apple pie,
put into the ovens, and the coal on top.

There was no range
There was no electric cooker that time
An oil lamp
maybe candles in the bedrooms
The pillowcases and sheets
were the flour bags, big bags
Eight stone you'd get into the bag
at that time
Eight stone for a family
There were no shops at that time,
no bakers
You had to bake every bit of bread
for the family
We did everything, we did indeed.
We had to knit everything
we had to knit instead of buying
for the family.

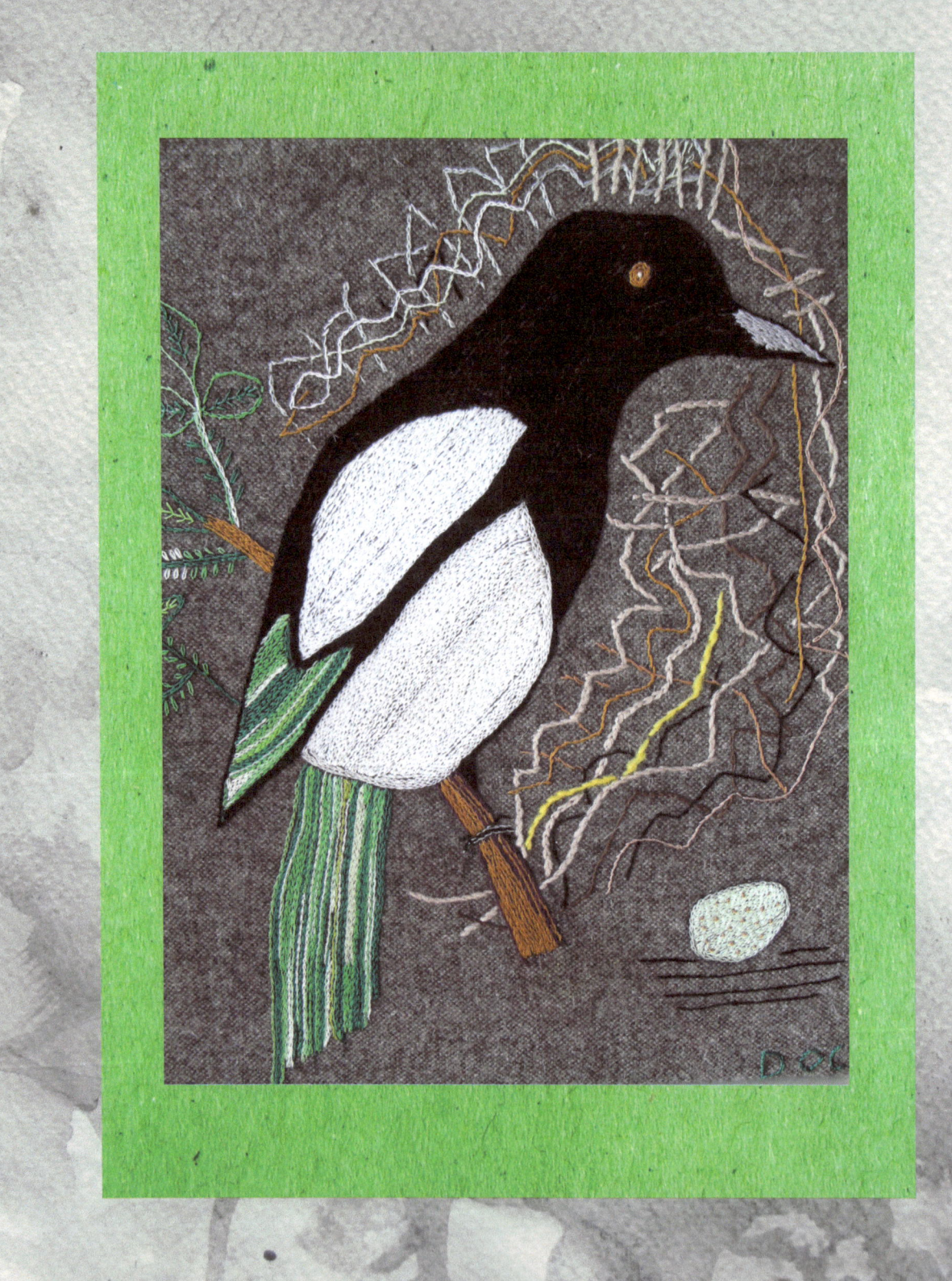

We had our jobs to do around the farm, and I'd work, I always have.
We had milking cows, we had a dairy farm at that time.
I went to school where the community centre is now. National
school—there was no secondary had that time by anyone.
As long as we could, we'd try to hold out on going to school with
shoes on, and all the children were the same. When it got cold
and frosty then we'd have the shoes on us.
At play hour then we'd be left out down to the strand in the
summertime, to pick cockles. The whole lot would go down to
the strand.

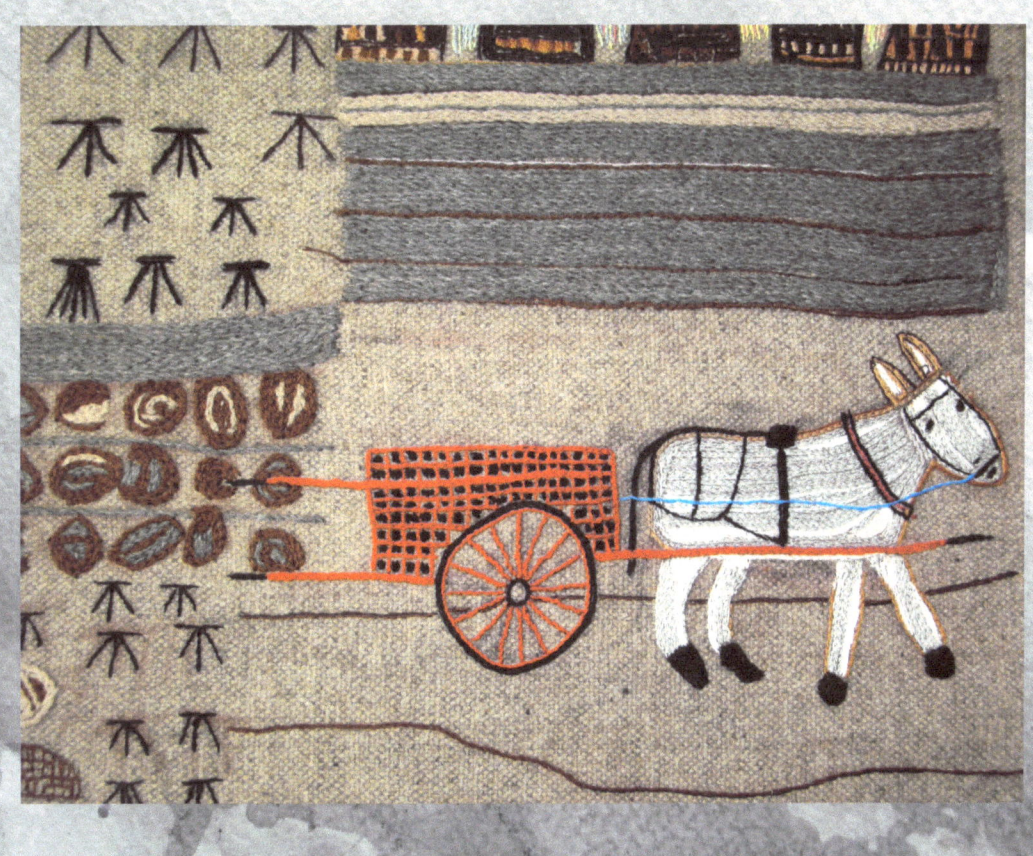

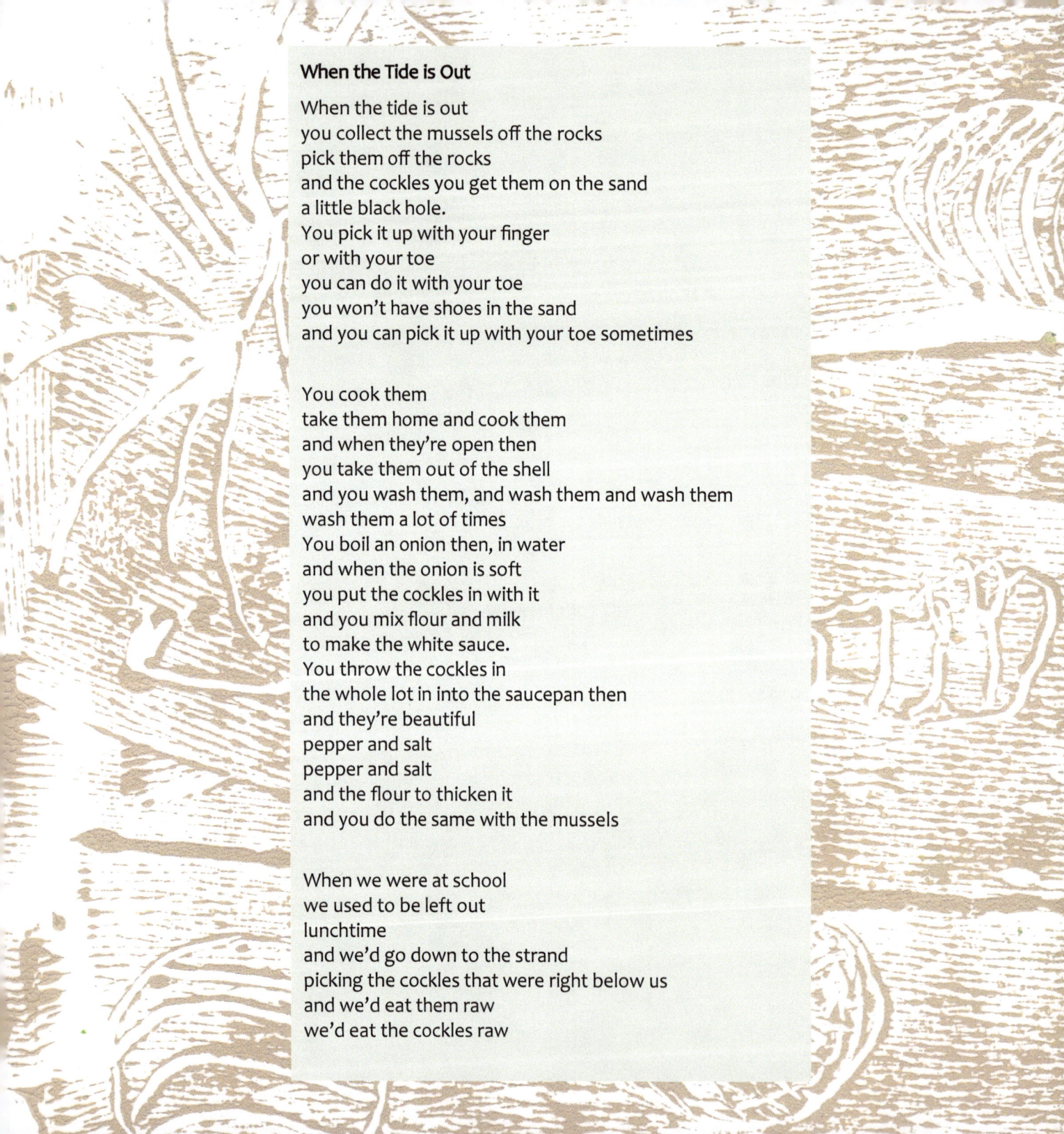

When the Tide is Out

When the tide is out
you collect the mussels off the rocks
pick them off the rocks
and the cockles you get them on the sand
a little black hole.
You pick it up with your finger
or with your toe
you can do it with your toe
you won't have shoes in the sand
and you can pick it up with your toe sometimes

You cook them
take them home and cook them
and when they're open then
you take them out of the shell
and you wash them, and wash them and wash them
wash them a lot of times
You boil an onion then, in water
and when the onion is soft
you put the cockles in with it
and you mix flour and milk
to make the white sauce.
You throw the cockles in
the whole lot in into the saucepan then
and they're beautiful
pepper and salt
pepper and salt
and the flour to thicken it
and you do the same with the mussels

When we were at school
we used to be left out
lunchtime
and we'd go down to the strand
picking the cockles that were right below us
and we'd eat them raw
we'd eat the cockles raw

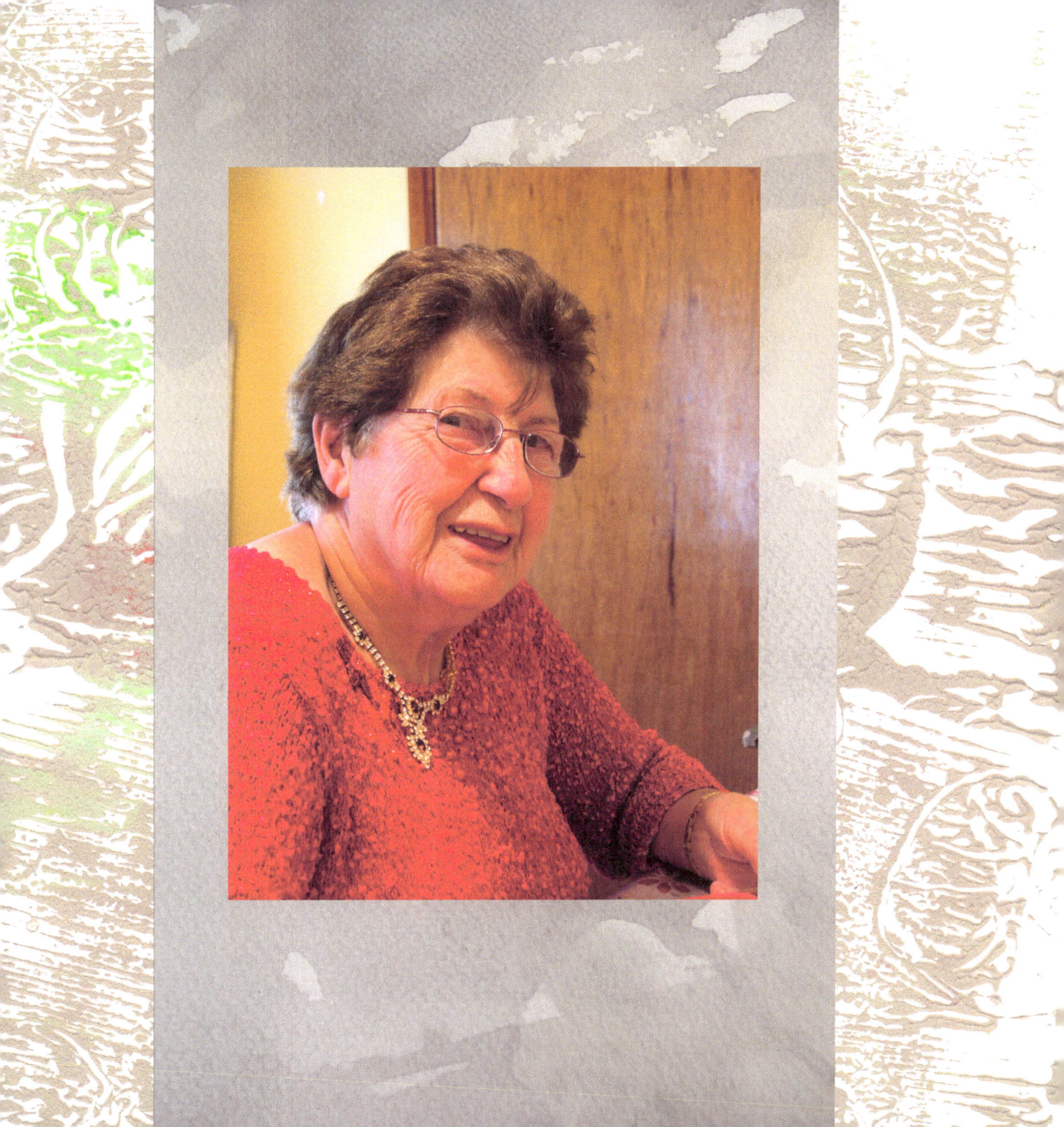

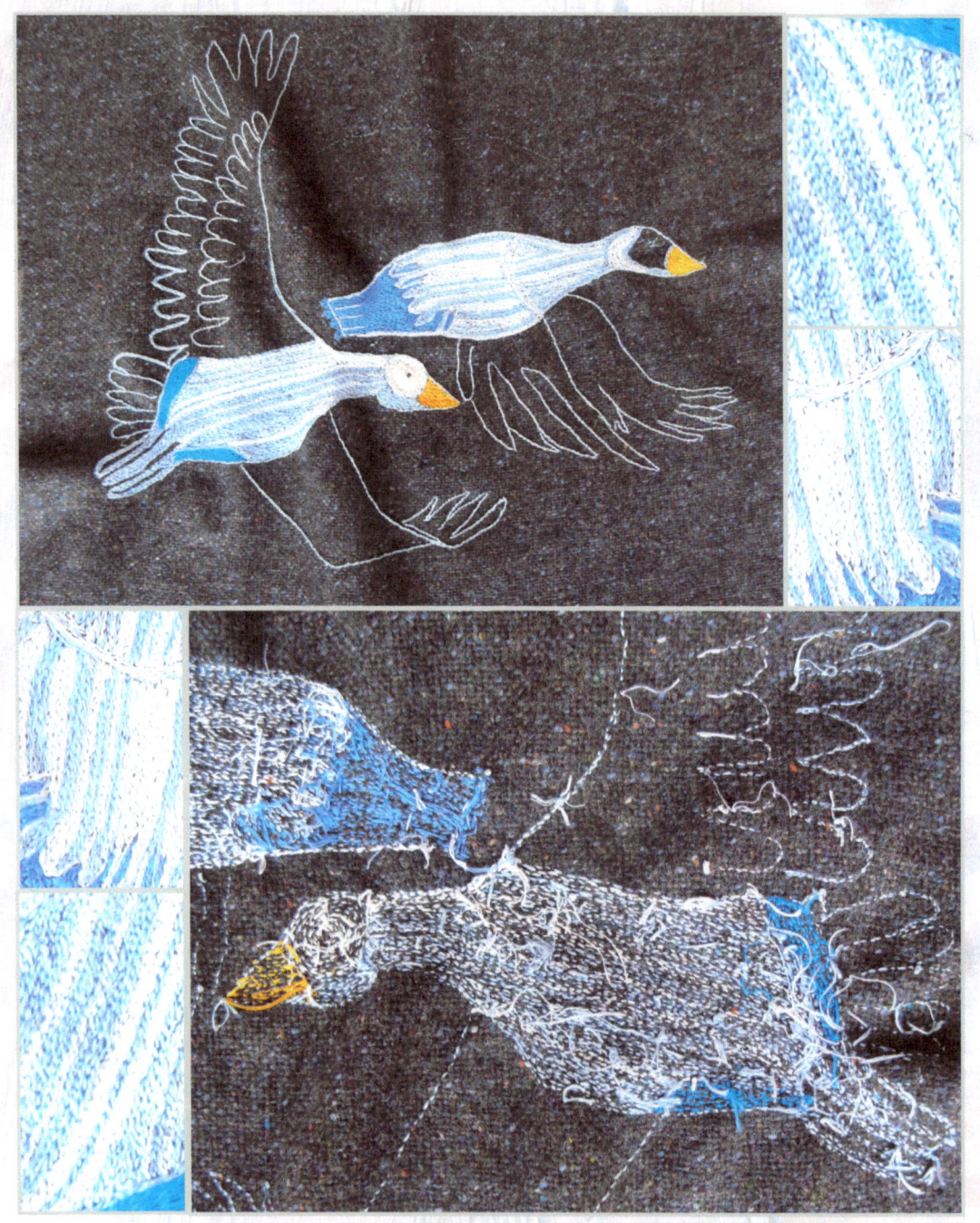

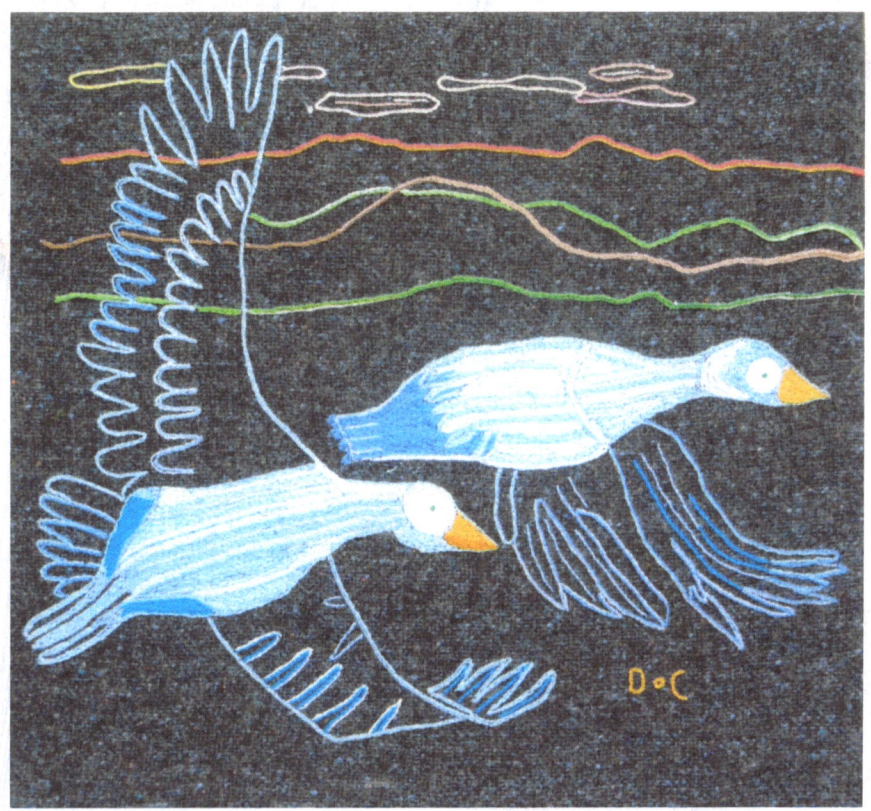

We did the knitting going to school, and darning. We did all our own knitting then, the jumpers and socks and everything. The wool didn't used to be in the small balls at all, that time. You'd put it up between two chairs, to make it into a ball. That's how the wool was long ago. We'd put it around two chairs, and we'd start winding. I'm all the time knitting; I knit for the young ones now, and darn. If they have a hole in their jumper, they'll bring it back here to me.

My mother used to crochet, she'd crochet beautiful spreads and everything, bedspreads. She didn't do embroidery. I never saw her doing embroidery, only the crochet and the knitting. The embroidery I just started myself.

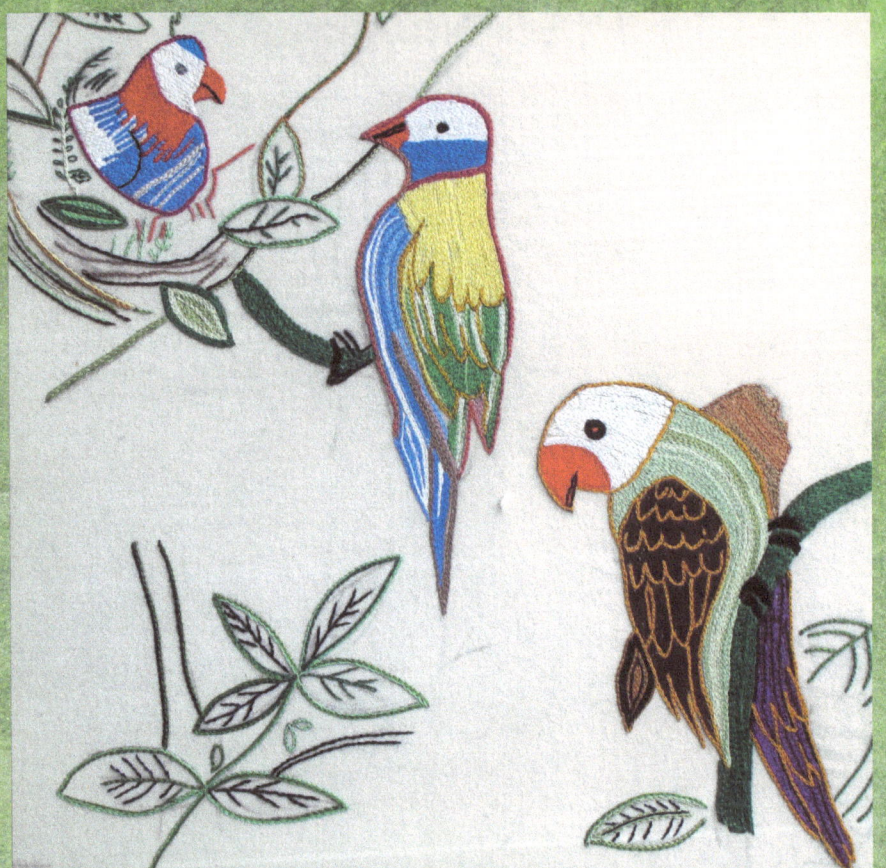

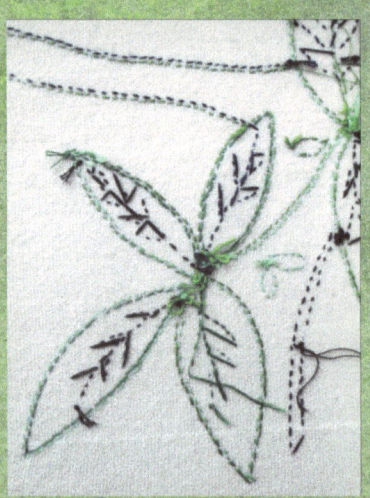

I got an embroidery pattern once
in a book, and I made a tablecloth
out of it, that was nearly the first one
I started.
'twas a beautiful thing, lovely flowers,
and a different pattern for the corner.
I don't know where it is now.

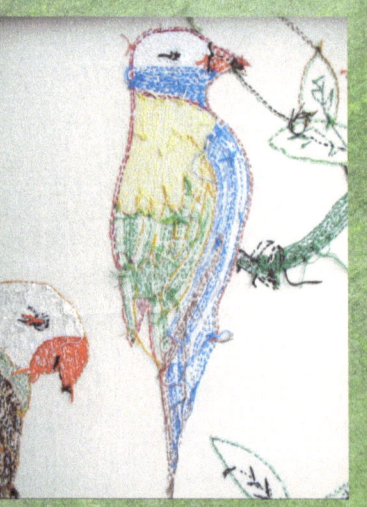

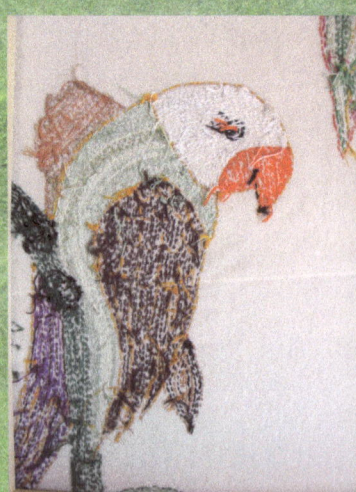

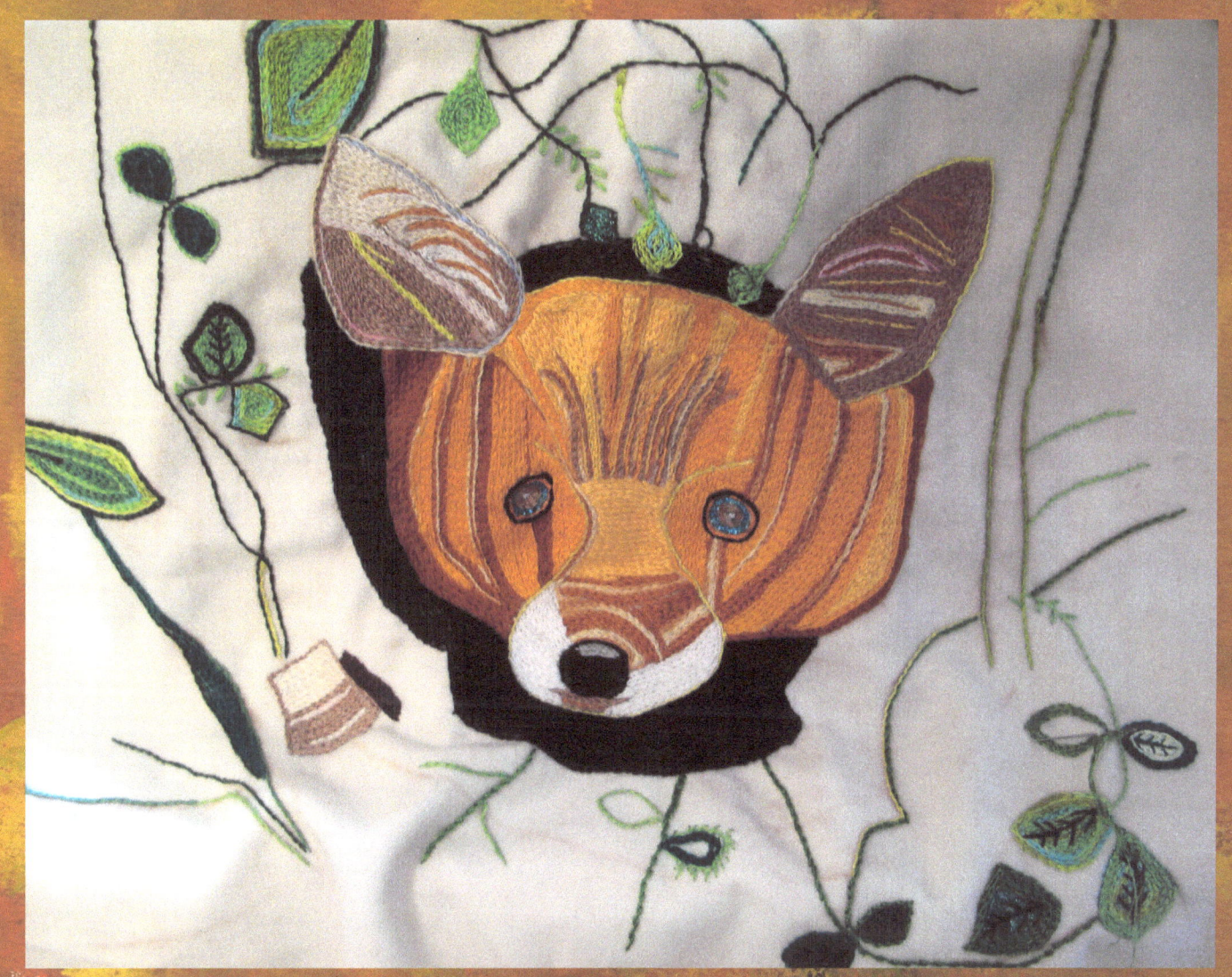

He was a fine fellow, the fox. He looked good with the glass and the frame.
There was a lot of work put into him too. The hours it took for him to come out,
I'd never count them now.

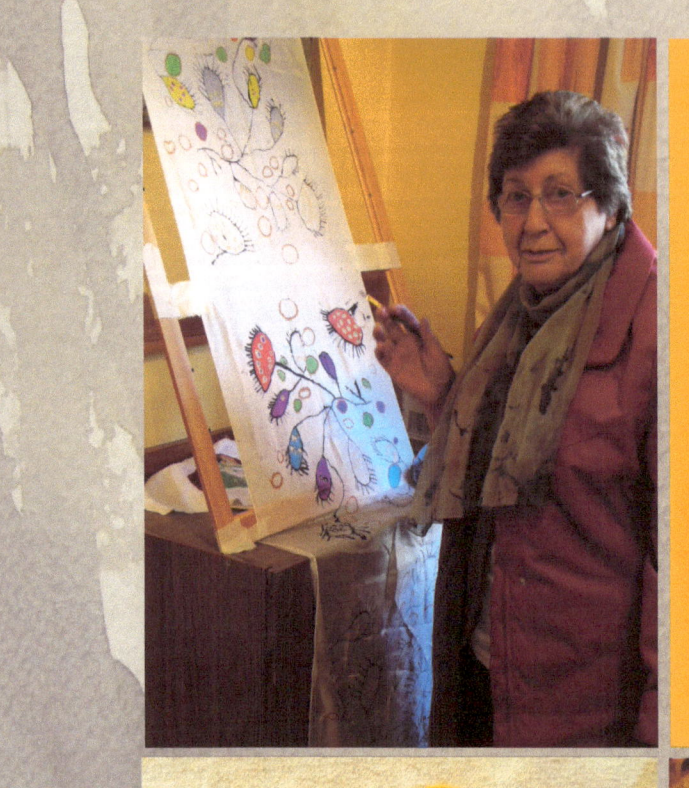

We had a class at the
community centre, and a teacher
would come to show us different
things. I was married that time.
We'd make trays, we'd get cane
and weave all around.
We'd get glass and we'd paint the
back of the glass different colours.
I like to be learning, to have
something to do.

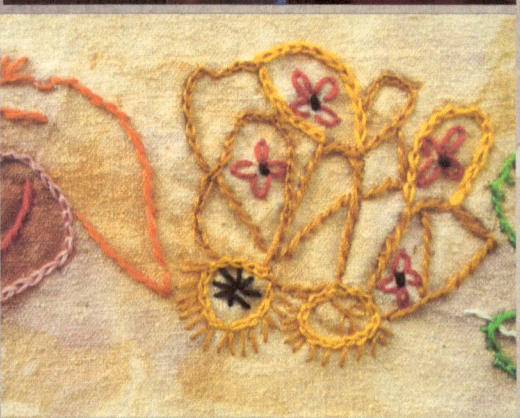

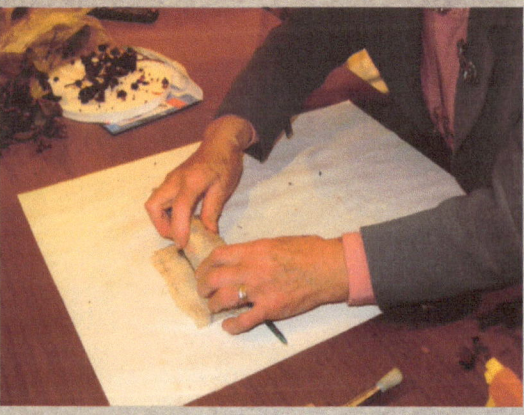

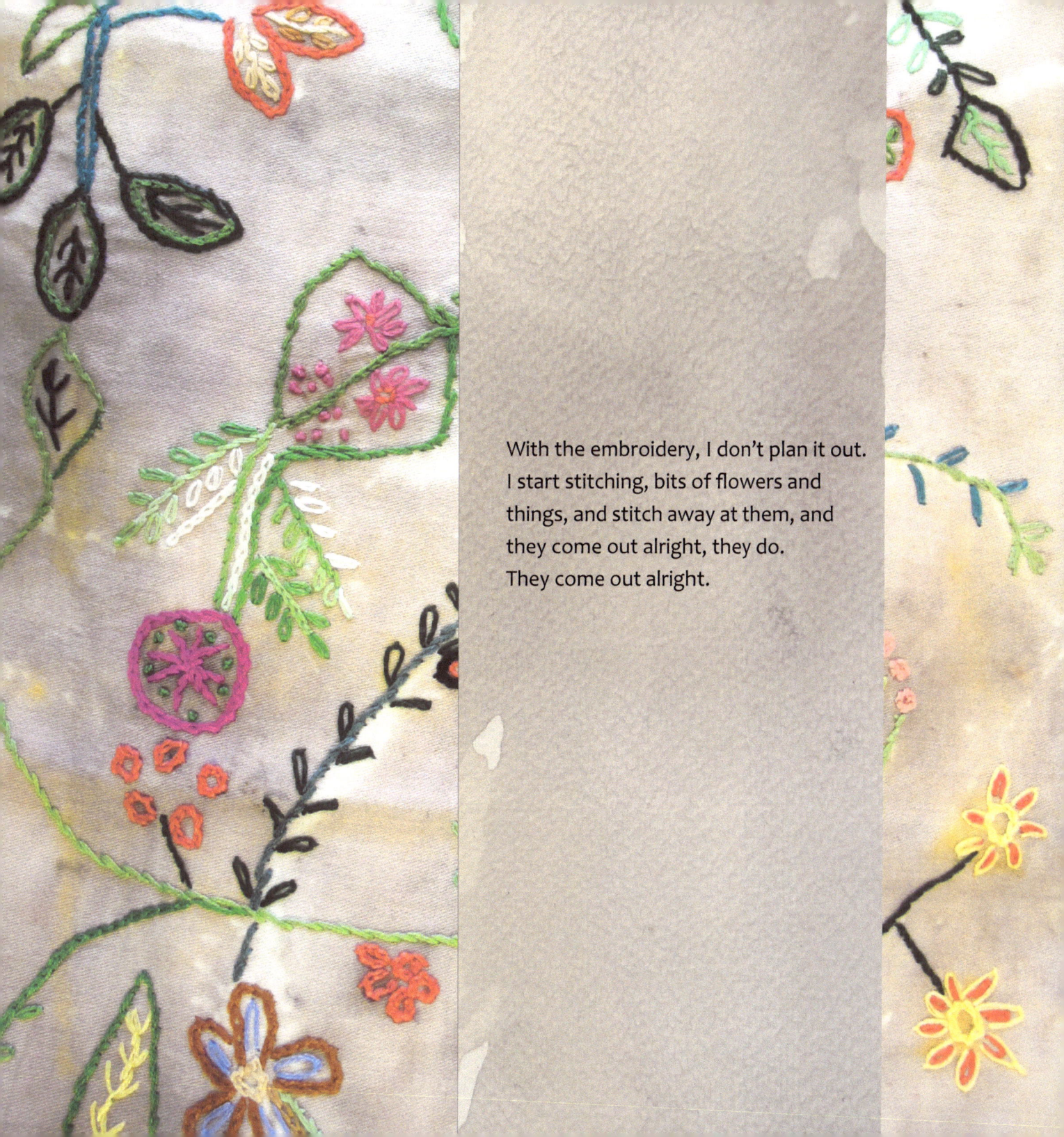

With the embroidery, I don't plan it out.
I start stitching, bits of flowers and
things, and stitch away at them, and
they come out alright, they do.
They come out alright.

I see a picture I like, and I go from there. Most of the pictures are from outside, from my life, anyway. We used to be outside, cutting turf, and saving the hay, in the fields saving the hay. 'twas alright in fine weather, but there'd be showers of rain always coming. My children were small that time and they all had their own pike, helping. There weren't many trousers worn by the women in that time, there wasn't; it was all done in dresses. Imagine that now.

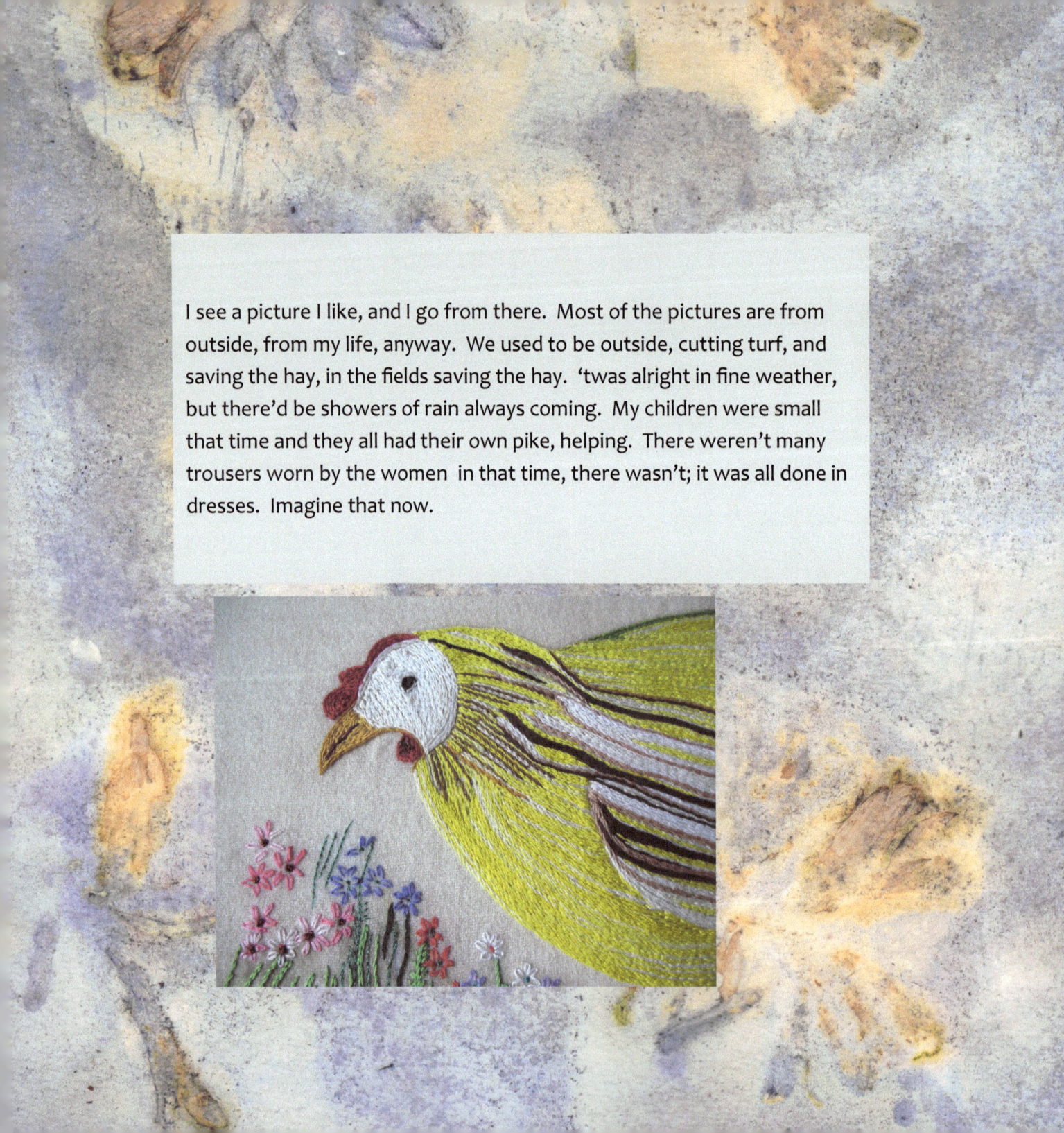

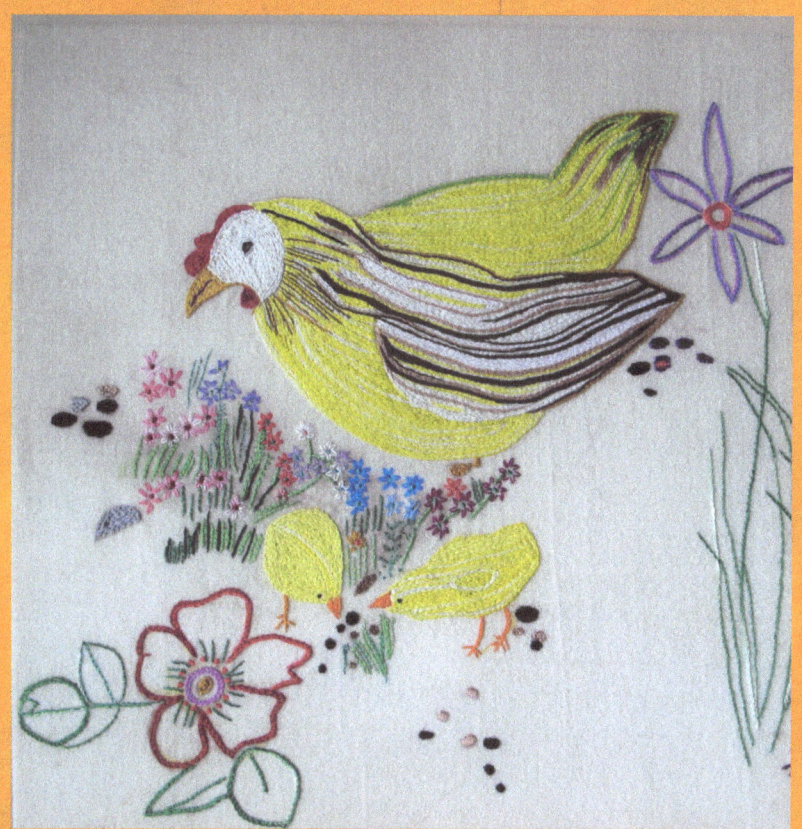

I'd make a basket out of butter, for the Stations.

You roll out two pieces first, with a rolling pin, and put one on the plate that way and another one on top of it, and put little balls of butter in to them. You'd get another ball then, and flatten it that way, and curl them sideways to make a leaf. You put the leaves all along, all around it. You put a plait for the handle, three pieces of butter, you'd roll them out long, and plait; you take it then and put it across the basket. You have it in and out of the fridge as you're making it.

But they used to make it for the Stations long ago, and they had no fridge, in my mother's time. Of course the house wasn't very hot at that time, the open fire, that's all they had. It was in some class they had, long ago, that my mother learned it. A long time ago. And I learned it from her. I made a beautiful basket of butter, and people were afraid to use the butter out of it; they didn't want to destroy the basket.

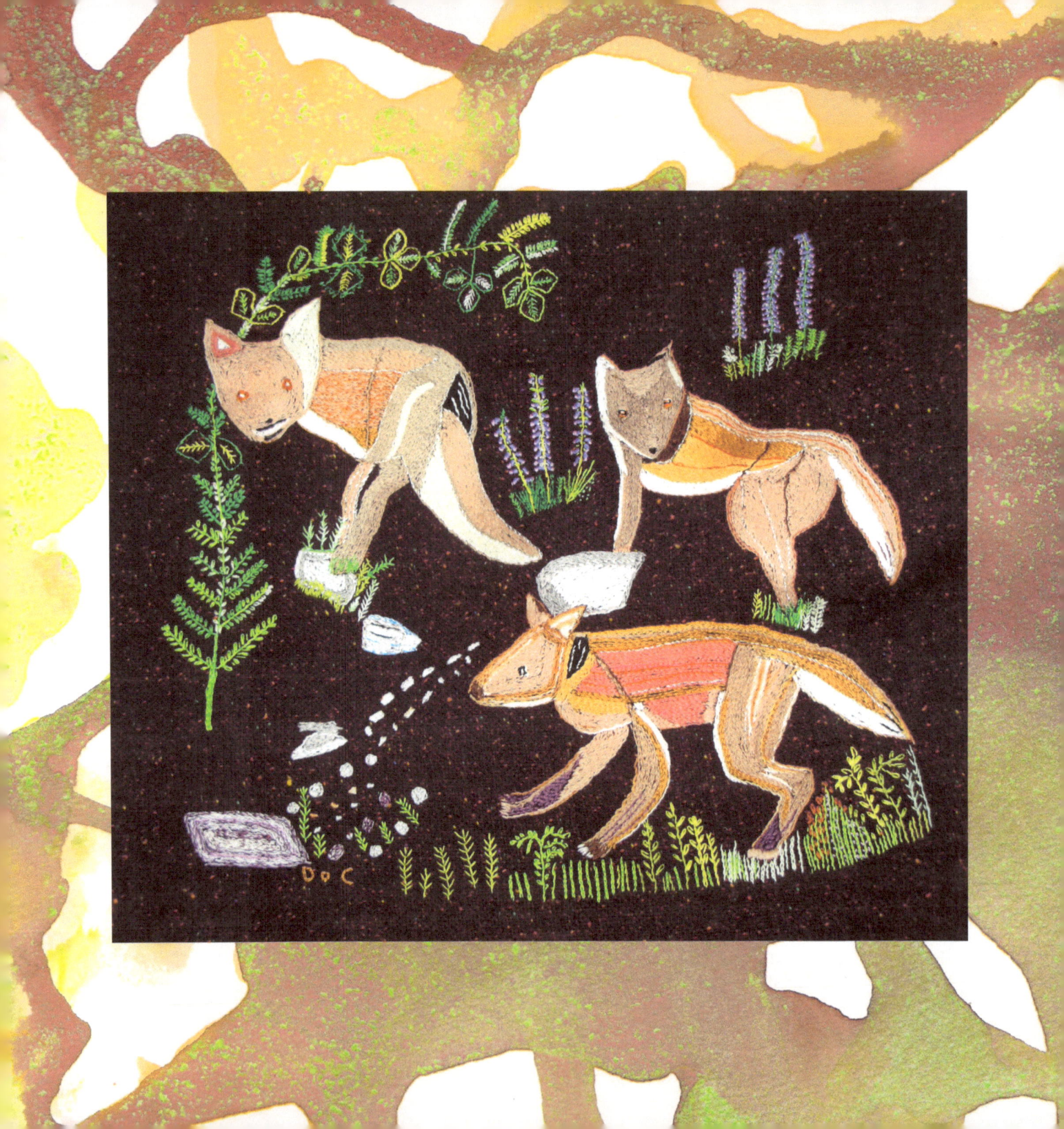

I'd do a bit of everything.
We did the set dancing, and the
plays, I was inside acting in the
plays. Sewing and knitting, by
night rehearsing for plays,
for competitions.
We won sometimes and failed
more times. But that's alright.
You won't win all the time.
I used to love the dancing; the
plays were nice too.
Now it's something for at home,
the embroidery and the knitting,
I like them both.
Anything to pass the time.

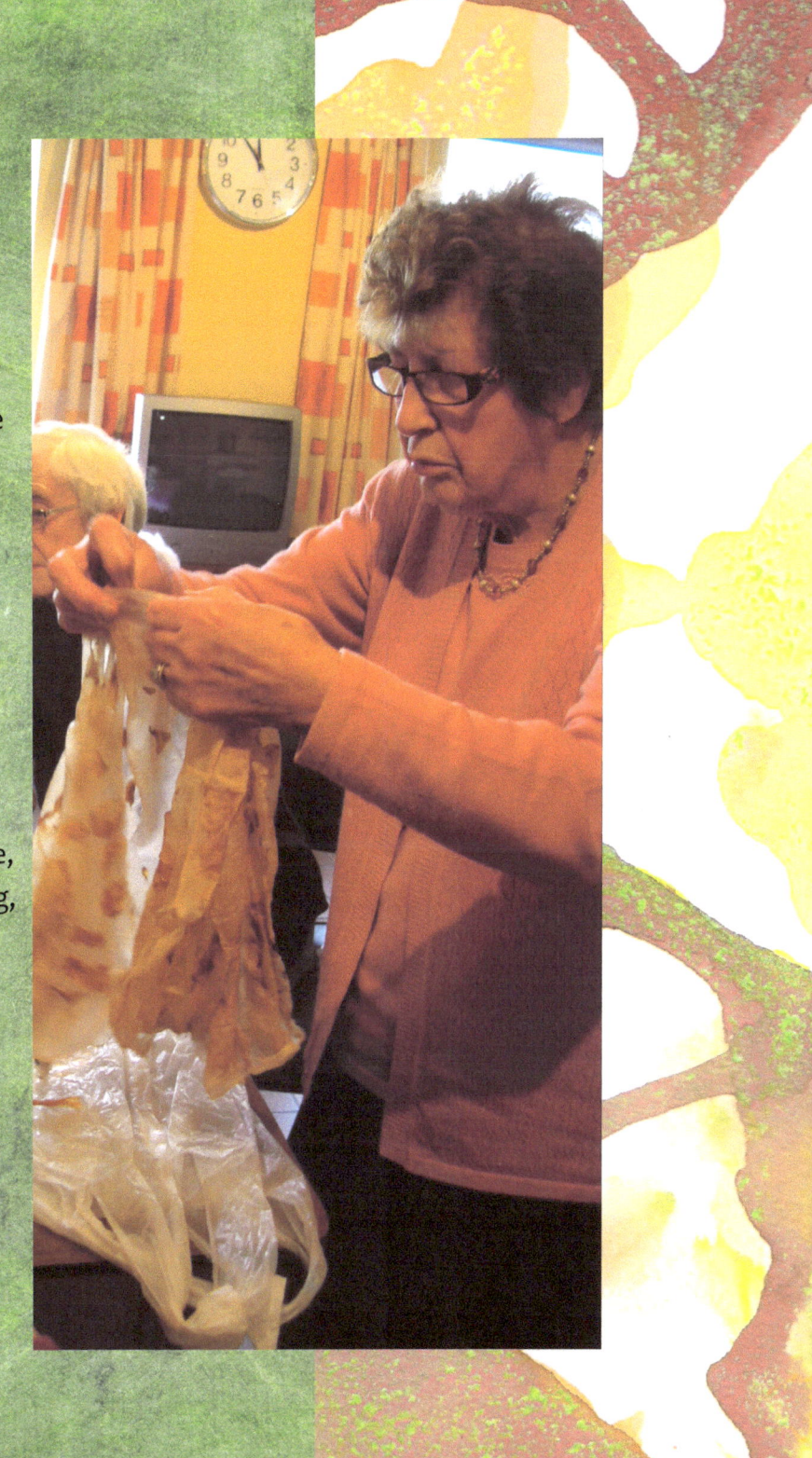

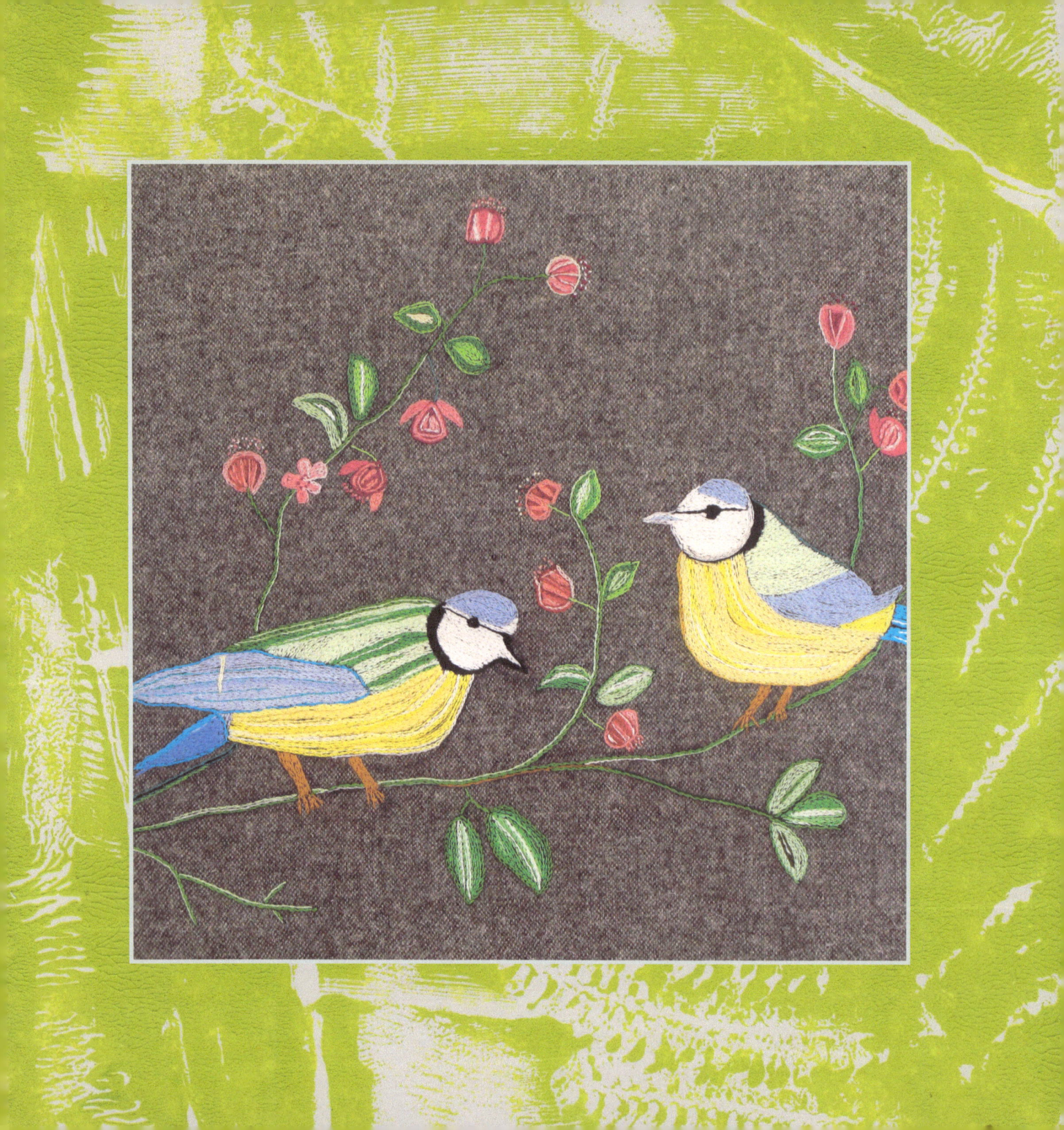

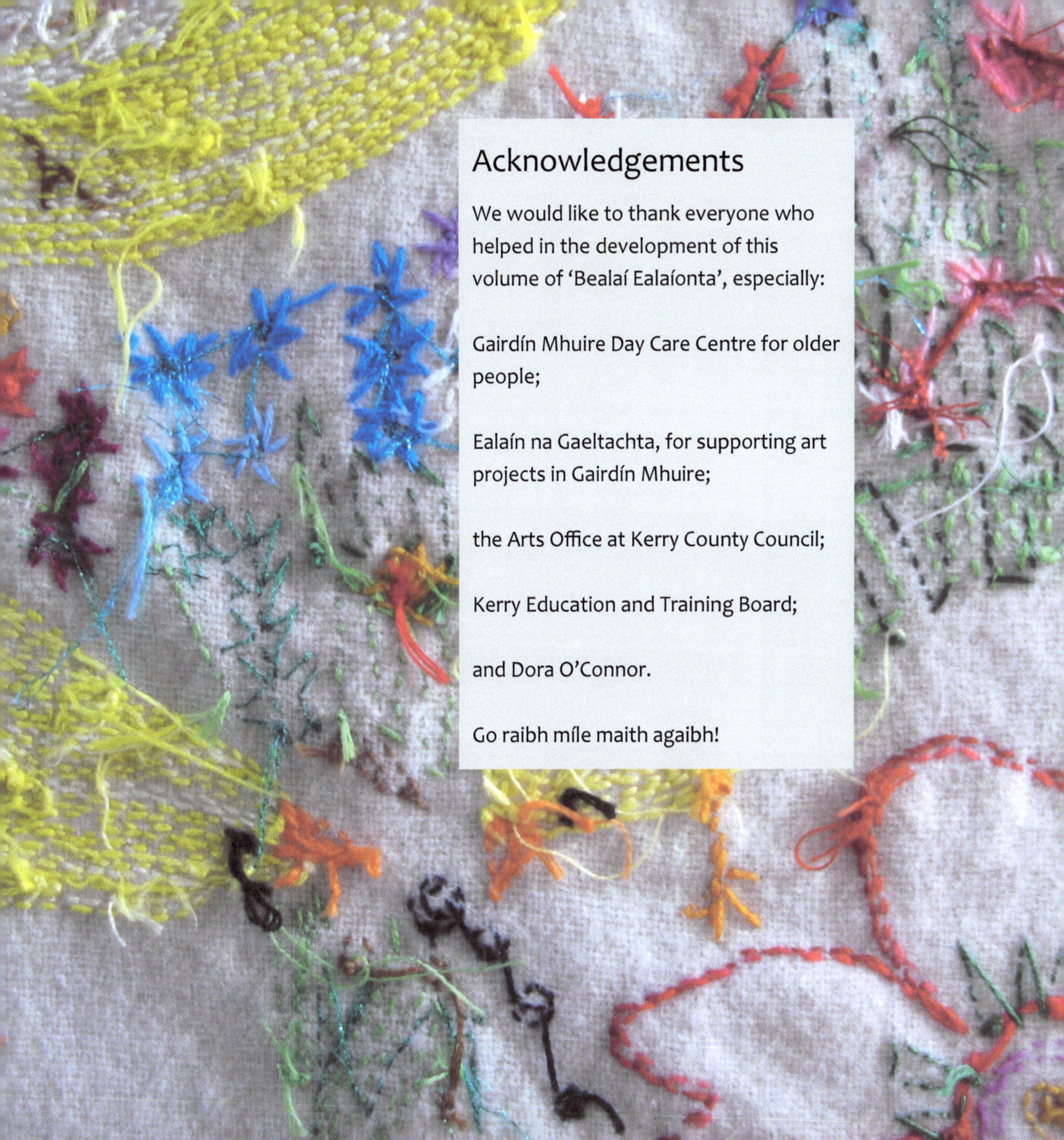

Acknowledgements

We would like to thank everyone who helped in the development of this volume of 'Bealaí Ealaíonta', especially:

Gairdín Mhuire Day Care Centre for older people;

Ealaín na Gaeltachta, for supporting art projects in Gairdín Mhuire;

the Arts Office at Kerry County Council;

Kerry Education and Training Board;

and Dora O'Connor.

Go raibh míle maith agaibh!

www.ingramcontent.com/pod-product-compliance
Lightning Source LLC
Chambersburg PA
CBHW050913180526
45159CB00007B/2897